# THE NATURE KIDS GUIDE TO

# SEA OTTERS

## DAVID ANDERSON

LP Media Inc. Publishing
Text copyright © 2026 by LP Media Inc.
All rights reserved.



For information address LP Media Inc. Publishing,
30012 Variolite St NW, Princeton MN 55371
www.lpmedia.org

Publication Data

Sea Otters
The Nature Kid's Guide to Sea Otters — First edition.

Summary: "Learn all about Sea Otters, the Nature Kid Way"
— Provided by publisher.

ISBN: 979-8-89818-106-2

[1. Sea Otters – Non-Fiction] I. Title.

Title: The Nature Kid's Guide to Sea Otters

# CONTENTS

# COLD COASTS

Sea otters have the thickest fur of any animal—up to one million hairs per square inch! They spend hours each day cleaning their fur to stay warm.

**Splash! A sea otter floats in chilly water. Its soft fur shines in the sun.**

Sea otters live along rocky coasts. They spend most of their time in the ocean. Cold water does not bother them because their thick fur keeps them warm.

Sea otters live in the North Pacific Ocean. They swim near shores where kelp forests grow. Kelp is a tall seaweed that sways in the waves.

Sea otters need clean, cold water to survive. They make their homes where food is plentiful. Rocky areas also give them places to find meals.

OTTER
OCEANS

# Swoosh! A sea otter dives below the waves near shore.

Sea otters live on both sides of the North Pacific Ocean. On one side, they swim along the coasts of California, Washington, and Alaska. On the other side, they live near Russia and Japan.

These otters rarely travel far from shore. They prefer shallow waters less than 100 feet deep where they can dive down to find food.

**Kelp** forests are their favorite habitat. The thick, swaying seaweed provides shelter from storms and hungry predators like sharks and orcas.

Sea otters can live their whole lives without ever touching dry land or coming to shore.

SIZE UP

**Whoosh! A sea otter floats on its back. Its fluffy fur rides the waves.**

Sea otters are one of the smallest **marine mammals**. But adult males can still grow to about four feet long. Females are a bit smaller.

Males weigh up to 65 pounds. Females weigh around 45 pounds. This smaller size helps them float easily.

Sea otters have loose skin and very thick fur. This fluffy fur puffs out and traps air. It makes them seem rounder in the water.

A newborn sea otter pup weighs only three to five pounds at birth. It cannot swim yet!

# FANTASTIC FUR

Unlike other ocean mammals, Sea otters have no blubber. Their fur alone keeps them warm in icy water.

**Rustle! A sea otter rubs its fur with both paws. It twists and rolls.**

Sea otters have the thickest fur of any mammal. One square inch holds about one million hairs. That is more hairs than you have on your entire head!

Their fur has two layers. The outer layer has long guard hairs. These keep water away from the skin. The inner layer is soft and dense, it traps dry air and keeps them warm without getting their skin wet.

Sea otters **groom** their fur every day. They roll and rub to add air bubbles. These tiny bubbles help them stay warm and float.

# SUPER SENSES

## Snap! A sea otter pops its head up. Its whiskers twitch.

Sea otters have amazing senses. Their whiskers feel tiny movements in the water. This helps them find food even when they cannot see.

Their eyes work well above and below water. They can spot danger from far away.

Sea otters also have good hearing.  Their small ears close tight when they dive, keeping water out while they search for food on the ocean floor.

Sea otters can hold their breath for up to five minutes!

# STAY SAFE

**Crunch! A sea otter cracks a clam on a rock. But it's eyes are watching for danger.**

Sea otters have ways to stay safe. They spend most of their time in the water. This keeps them away from land **predators**.

Sea otters rest in kelp forests. They wrap kelp around their bodies. The seaweed holds them in place and hides them.

They also stay in groups called rafts. Many eyes watch for danger together.

Sea otters hold hands while sleeping so they don't drift apart in the water.

# SEAFOOD SNACKS

**Chomp! A sea otter bites into a purple sea urchin.**

Sea otters eat many kinds of seafood. They munch on clams, crabs, and snails. Sea urchins are one of their favorite treats.

Sea otters eat a lot each day. They need food equal to about one quarter of their body weight. This keeps them warm in cold water.

All this crunchy food requires strong teeth. Their back teeth are flat and wide, which helps them crush hard shells easily.

Sea otters eat over 40 different sea creatures. Each otter has its own favorites: some prefer crabs while others love abalone!

17

# DIVE DEEP

FUN
FACT!

Sea otters close their ears and
nostrils underwater to keep water
out while diving.

**Plop! A sea otter drops beneath the surface. It kicks down deep.**

Sea otters are great divers. They swim down to the ocean floor to find food. Most dives last about one minute.

Sea otters can dive up to 350 feet deep. They use their back feet to push through the water. They keep their front paws tucked close to their chest.

On the bottom, they search with their paws. They feel under rocks and in sand. They grab prey and tuck it under their arm.

Then they swim back up to eat at the surface.

WATCH OUT

## Screech! A hungry eagle perches on a branch. Danger is near.

Sea otters face dangers in the ocean. Sharks and killer whales hunt them in the water. These large predators swim fast and strike quickly.

On land, sea otters must watch for other hunters. Eagles can grab small pups from the surface. Coyotes attack otters on the shore.

Sea otters stay alert to survive. Living in groups helps them spot threats faster.

Sea otters wrap themselves in kelp to rest safely in place while they sleep.

# QUICK ESCAPE

# Zoom! A sea otter speeds through the water, darting away fast.

Sea otters can hold their breath for up to five minutes. This lets them twist and turn deep underwater. Their flexible bodies help them change direction fast.

When scared, sea otters can swim nearly 6 miles per hour. They can also dive down quickly when they need to hide.

Some otters escape to kelp forests. They wrap up in seaweed to camoflauge themselves.

Sea otters do somersaults and barrel rolls underwater to confuse predators.

SWIM STARS

# Click! A sea otter cracks open a clam while floating.

Sea otters are strong swimmers. Their bodies are built for life in the ocean.

Sea otters use their wide, flat back feet like flippers. They kick both feet together to push forward. Their front paws are small with retractable claws, perfect for grabbing food and grooming their fur

Their flat tails help them steer. This lets sea otters spin, roll, and turn quickly in the water.

Sea otters can swim on their backs or their bellies. They often float belly-up to rest.

# DAY DRIFTERS

**Squeak! A sea otter yawns and stretches as it drifts slowly on the waves.**

Sea otters spend most of their day floating. They rest on their backs in the water. While floating, they groom their fur many times each day.

Sea otters eat, sleep, and play while floating. They rarely go on land. The ocean is their home.

Otters often nap during the day. They close their eyes and bob gently on the waves.

Sea otters sometimes spin in circles while floating to scratch hard-to-reach spots on their bodies.

28

## Bark! Sea otters bob together in a group. They drift along side by side.

Sea otters often float in groups. A group of sea otters is called a **raft**. Rafts can have just a few otters or over one hundred.

Otters in a raft sometimes hold paws. This keeps them from drifting apart while they sleep.

Male and female otters often form separate rafts.

The largest raft ever seen had over 2,000 sea otters floating together in Alaska.

# FINDING LOVE

## Chirp! A male sea otter swims near a female otter.

Sea otters can mate at any time of year. However, males and females do not stay together after mating.

Male sea otters swim through female rafts to find a mate. A male may stay near a female for a few days.

After mating, females can have one pup each year. Most sea otter pups are born in the spring or early summer.

**Male sea otters are ready to mate at about five or six years old. Females mature a bit earlier.**

PRECIOUS PUPS
DID YOU KNOW?
Mother otters blow air into their pup's fur to make it fluffy. This trapped air helps the baby float!

## Squawk! A fluffy sea otter pup floats in the kelp.

Baby sea otters are called pups. Newborn pups have thick, fluffy fur. This fur helps them float on the water.

Pups cannot swim at first. They ride on their mother's chest. She keeps them warm and dry above the waves.

As pups grow, they learn to dive and find food. Young otters stay with their mothers for about six months.

When pups leave their mothers, they must survive on their own. Young females often stay near where they were born. Young males swim off to find new territory, sometimes traveling many miles away.

# MOM KNOWS

DID YOU KNOW?
Mothers can spend up to 14 hours a day hunting for food for their pups.

34

## Grunt! A mother sea otter grooms her fluffy pup gently.

Mother sea otters work hard to raise their pups. They spend hours each day grooming their babies. This clean fur keeps pups warm and floating.

Mothers teach pups many skills. They show them how to dive for food. They also teach them to crack open shells.

A mother wraps her pup in kelp to keep it safe. She dives below to hunt while her pup waits. She returns to feed and care for her pup.

36

**Rumble! Waves crash on a rocky shore. A lone sea otter looks around.**

Sea otters face many dangers today. Oil spills can hurt their fur. Without clean fur, otters cannot stay warm.

Pollution harms the ocean. Trash and chemicals make otters sick.

Climate change warms the water. This affects the food otters need. Kelp forests can die in warm seas.

By 1911, hunters reduced sea otters to just 2,000. Laws now protect them. About 150,000 live in the wild today!

# HELPING HANDS

# A wet pup rests in gentle hands. At the rescue center, workers give orphaned otters a second chance.

Sea otters almost disappeared long ago. Hunters wanted their soft fur. Very few otters were left.

Today, laws protect sea otters. These laws stop most people from hunting them. This helps otter numbers grow.

Scientists also work to help sea otters. They track where otters live. Rescue groups help sick or hurt otters get better too.

Rescue centers raise orphaned otter pups and teach them to find food before release.

# GLOSSARY

**kelp**
A very tall seaweed that grows in the ocean.

**marine mammals**
Animals with fur that live in the ocean and breathe air.

**groom**
To clean and take care of fur by rubbing and brushing it.

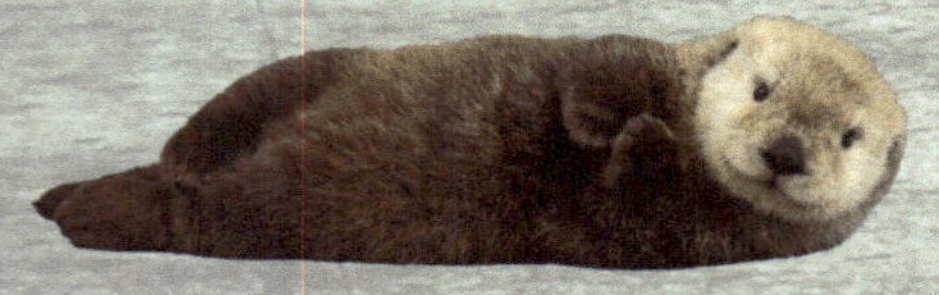

**predators**
Animals that hunt and eat other animals.

**raft**
A group of sea otters floating together in the water.